# EXPLORERS

# James
# Cook

### Kristin Petrie

ABDO
Publishing Company

## visit us at
## www.abdopub.com

Published by ABDO Publishing Company, 4940 Viking Drive, Edina, Minnesota 55435.
Copyright © 2004 by Abdo Consulting Group, Inc. International copyrights reserved in all
countries. No part of this book may be reproduced in any form without written permission from
the publisher.

Printed in the United States.

Cover Photos: Corbis
Interior Photos: Corbis pp. 5, 7, 8, 9, 11, 12, 13, 14, 15, 17, 18, 19, 21, 24, 25, 27, 28, 29

Series Coordinator: Stephanie Hedlund
Editors: Kate A. Conley, Kristin Van Cleaf
Art Direction & Cover Design: Neil Klinepier
Interior Design & Maps: Dave Bullen

### Library of Congress Cataloging-in-Publication Data

Petrie, Kristin, 1970-
   James Cook / Kristin Petrie.
      p. cm. -- (Explorers)
   Includes index.
   Summary: An introduction to the life of the eighteenth-century British explorer and navigator
who is famous for his three great voyages of exploration in the South Pacific Ocean, as well as
for his attempt to find a Northwest passage across the North American continent.
   ISBN 1-59197-596-4
   1. Cook, James, 1728-1779--Juvenile literature. 2. Explorers--Great Britain--Biography--
Juvenile literature. 3. Voyages around the world--Juvenile literature. [1. Cook, James, 1728-
1779. 2. Explorers. 3. Voyages around the world. 4. Oceania--Discovery and exploration--
British.] I. Title.

G420.C62P48 2004
910'.92--dc22
   [B]                                                                                    2003062926

# Contents

# James Cook

Can you imagine sailing around the world? Amazingly, James Cook did this, twice! Captain Cook was a British navigator. He has been called one of the world's greatest explorers. Cook led three extraordinary voyages through the Pacific Ocean. One was even done in a leaky boat.

On his voyages, Cook mapped Australia's unexplored eastern coast and New Zealand. He introduced the world to the Hawaiian Islands. And, his work led to the founding of European colonies throughout the Pacific Ocean.

Captain Cook proved the vastness of the Pacific Ocean. It was more than twice as large as the Atlantic! This knowledge enlarged the estimates about Earth's size. Let's join Captain Cook on his adventures.

| | 1451 | | 1485 | |
| | Christopher Columbus born | | Hernán Cortés born | |

| 1450 | | 1460 | | 1491 |
| John Cabot born | | Vasco da Gama born | | Jacques Cartier born |

**James Cook**

*1492*
Columbus's first voyage west for Spain

*1496*
Cabot's first voyage for England

*1493*
Columbus's second voyage, attempted to colonize Hispaniola

# Early Years

James Cook was born on October 27, 1728. He was the second of Grace and James Cook's seven children. The Cook family lived in Marton-in-Cleaveland, a small farming village in England.

Young James's father was a poor farm laborer. The family could not afford to send their children to school. James was very bright, however, and his father's employer noticed this. So, he paid for James to go to elementary school.

James studied basic subjects such as reading and writing. He showed a special skill in math. When James was about 16 or 17, he was sent to work in the nearby fishing village of Staithes. The activities in this seafaring community began to shape James's life. He developed a passion for the sea.

In 1746, James was an **apprentice** to John Walker in Whitby, England. Walker and his brother owned a **fleet** of

**1497**
Cabot's second voyage, discovered the Grand Banks; da Gama was first to sail around Africa to India

**1496 or 1497**
Hernando de Soto born

**1498**
Cabot's third voyage, may have died; Columbus's third voyage

colliers.  These strong, sturdy coal ships could carry large loads.  James learned how to expertly pilot them.  This experience would help him on future voyages.

Whitby, England, is still a bustling port.

*1502*
Columbus's fourth voyage; da Gama's second voyage

*1506*
Columbus died

*1504*
Cortés sailed to the West Indies

# Navy Man

James was a hard worker. While living in Whitby, he taught himself about navigation, astronomy, and mathematics. In 1755, James was offered the position of **master** of his own collier. But by then, James knew he wanted to do more than haul freight.

James turned down the offer and volunteered for the British Royal Navy. This was a surprising decision. Being a sailor in the navy was an awful job. In fact, it was so bad that men were often impressed into service. This meant that they were kidnapped and forced into the job!

**James Cook was in the Royal Navy for 24 years.**

The Seven Years' War broke out between Britain and France in 1756. James was sent on the *Eagle* to patrol the northern Atlantic Ocean. For two years, he served as an ordinary sailor.

1511
Cortés helped take over Cuba

1510
Francisco Vásquez de Coronado born

1514
De Soto went to the New World

# Would You?

Would you volunteer to join the navy when others were being kidnapped to do it? Why do you think Cook chose this profession?

Cook taught himself how to read a map and navigate a ship.

James's sailing and leadership abilities made him stand apart. He quickly made his way up the ranks. By 1757, James was a **master** of a **survey** vessel.

James had several assignments at this rank. For one, James and the crew were sent to Canada to chart the St. Lawrence River. His exceptional work helped the British navy take over Quebec City.

On another assignment, James surveyed the coasts of Newfoundland and Labrador. His drawings and maps were extremely **accurate**. His superiors began to take notice of this talented young man.

James returned to England and met Elizabeth Batts. She was the daughter of a wealthy family from Barking, England. The couple married on December 21, 1762.

Despite James's life at sea, he and Elizabeth had six children. During James's absences, Elizabeth cared for them. She faced many hardships. She even lived to see the deaths of all six of her children. Elizabeth died in 1835.

*1524*
Da Gama's third voyage, died in Cochin, India

*1519–1521*
Cortés conquered the Aztec Empire and claimed Mexico for Spain

*1532*
De Soto helped attack the Inca Empire

Quebec City was built by the French in 1608. James Cook's maps helped the English take over the city in 1763.

# Astronomer

While charting Newfoundland in 1766, Cook wrote a report on a solar eclipse. It gained him recognition in the scientific community. The report was noticed by the Royal Society. It is one of the oldest scientific groups in Europe.

In 1768, the Royal Society was looking for someone to lead an exciting expedition. It decided that Cook was the perfect man for the job.

Astronomer Edmond Halley had predicted the planet Venus would cross in front of the sun in 1769. Scientists wanted to observe this event from several places. Their calculations would be used to determine the distance between Earth and the sun.

On August 25, 1768, Cook set sail for one of these points. We know it as Tahiti.

Edmond Halley

1534
Cartier's first voyage for France

1539–1542
De Soto explored La Florida

1533
De Soto helped take over Cuzco

1535
Cartier's second voyage

The *Endeavour* carried Cook's crew of 85 sailors and nine scientists. The collier was loaded down with **ammunition**, scientific equipment, and enough food to last two years.

Eight months later, the *Endeavour* reached Tahiti. In June 1769, Cook, his crew, and the scientists watched in amazement as Venus crossed the sun. Following this spectacular occurrence, they explored and mapped the island's coast.

Cook observed the eclipse from this bay in Tahiti. He named it Point Venus.

# A New Search

In mid-July 1769, the second part of Cook's expedition began. From Tahiti, the crew searched for other islands in the area. Then, Cook began a quest to find an entirely undiscovered continent. It supposedly existed very far to the south in the Pacific and Atlantic oceans.

For centuries, scientists had talked about a possible continent at the bottom of the world. Geographers even drew maps featuring a huge continent far to the south. It was thought to stretch into warmer zones near South America, Asia, and Africa.

Other explorers had sailed the southern waters looking for hints of the continent. They had reported land in different places. So after leaving Tahiti, Cook searched throughout the South Pacific for these lands. Bad weather eventually forced him to turn back.

**Cook in uniform**

1541
Cartier's third voyage, attempted to colonize Canada; Cortés volunteered to fight against Algiers

1540
Coronado set out to find the Seven Cities of Cíbola; Francis Drake born

## Would You?

Would you search for a continent that may not exist? Why or why not?

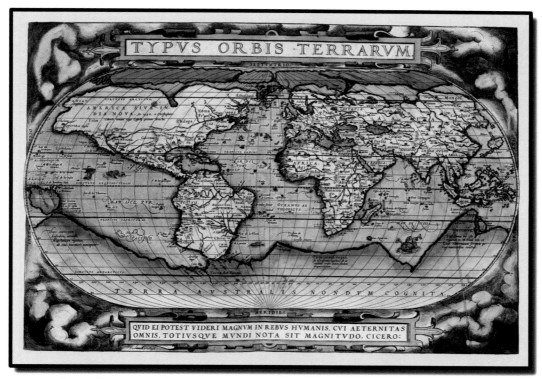

**TYPVS ORBIS TERRARVM.**

QVID EI POTEST VIDERI MAGNVM IN REBVS HVMANIS, CVI AETERNITAS OMNIS, TOTIVSQVE MVNDI NOTA SIT MAGNITVDO. CICERO:

**Though Antarctica had not yet been found, maps in the 1700s often showed a large continent in the Southern Hemisphere.**

*1547*
Cortés died

*1557*
Cartier died

*1542*
Coronado returned to New Spain; de Soto died

*1554*
Coronado died

*1566*
Drake's first voyage to the New World

# Charting Islands

From the South Pacific, Cook headed back to the northwest. Now, he looked for a land Dutch sailors had spotted years before. It was named New Zealand.

In October, the *Endeavour* landed at a bay on New Zealand's North Island. Here, Cook met the islanders, the Maori. The natives were fearful of the intruders, so Cook and his crew did not go inland.

For six months, the *Endeavour* sailed around New Zealand's North and South islands. Cook carefully charted the islands' coastlines. From New Zealand, Cook turned his ship to the west again.

Two weeks later, the *Endeavour* reached New Holland, or Australia. Dutch explorers had also discovered this continent. Cook and his crew, however, were the first Europeans to land on Australia's eastern coast.

The *Endeavour* sailed from the southeastern tip of Australia up the coast. Cook wanted to sail close to the

*1567*
Drake's second voyage

*1577*
Drake began a worldwide voyage, was first Englishman to sail the Pacific Ocean

*1570 and 1572*
Drake terrorized the Spanish in the New World

shore to chart the coastline. However, he and the crew did not know about the many **shoals** and reefs along the coast.

The *Endeavour* sailed right into the Great Barrier Reef and was nearly shipwrecked. The crew was forced to land. They stayed for two months while repairing the hull. During this time, they learned about Australia's land, plants, and animals. Can you imagine the first sighting of a kangaroo?

In early August the *Endeavour*, still leaking, set sail again. Cook carefully navigated the reefs. After four months of charting 2,000 miles (3,200 km) of coastline, the crew reached

**This monument stands at Botany Bay, Australia, where Cook landed.**

the northeast tip of Australia. Cook claimed the entire eastern coast for Britain. He named it New South Wales.

Once clear of the reefs, the *Endeavour* began its long journey home. The crew's first stop was in Batavia, Indonesia. There, the ship underwent repairs.

One of Cook's greatest accomplishments was keeping his crew healthy. He had prevented the usual illnesses, including **scurvy**, for nearly three years. However, conditions in Batavia were so bad that many of Cook's party became ill and died. Finally, the expedition reached England on July 12, 1771.

**Cook's crew landed to repair the *Endeavour*.**

1588
Drake helped England win the Battle of Gravelines against Spain's Invincible Armada

1581
Drake knighted by Queen Elizabeth I

1596
Drake died

**Would You?**

Would you continue charting a coast while sailing in a leaking boat? Do you think Cook was foolish to keep mapping the area? Why or why not?

**Cook claimed the coast of Australia for England.**

*1728*
James Cook born

*1765*
Boone journeyed to Florida

*1768*
Cook sailed for Tahiti

*1734*
Daniel Boone born

*1767*
Boone explored Kentucky

# A Cold Journey

In 1771, Cook was chosen to lead another mission in search of the southern continent. If he found it, he was to claim it for Britain. Cook and his crew left Plymouth, England, on July 13, 1772. On board the *Resolution* and the *Adventure* was a team of scientists, astronomers, and artists.

The ships sailed far into the southern parts of the oceans. They were looking for a place called Cape Circumcision. Earlier sailors had thought it was a part of the southern continent. Cook found no sign of it. He concluded that it had been a huge iceberg rather than land.

While searching for Cape Circumcision, Cook and his crew became the first people to cross the Antarctic Circle. In January 1773, the ships neared the continent of Antarctica. Cook was so close! However, ice and harsh weather kept him from seeing the very continent he had been searching for.

In 1773, Cook gave up his search for the mysterious continent. Before he returned to England, Cook stopped at several small islands near New Zealand. Other explorers had landed on these islands in the South Pacific before. However, Cook was the first to chart them **accurately**.

**A chronometer from the 1800s**

## THE CHRONOMETER

*Cook's second voyage had another purpose. The crew was to test out a new navigational instrument called a chronometer. This instrument allowed navigators to determine their longitude by using a clock.*

*Before this instrument, clocks were inaccurate at sea. Temperature and the ship's motion affected them. The chronometer had suspended mechanisms and an airtight case. These improvements would help captains determine their location and speed while at sea.*

*1778*
Cook became the first European to record Hawaiian Islands; Boone captured by Shawnee

*1775*
Boone cut the Wilderness Road from Virginia to Kentucky

*1779*
Cook died

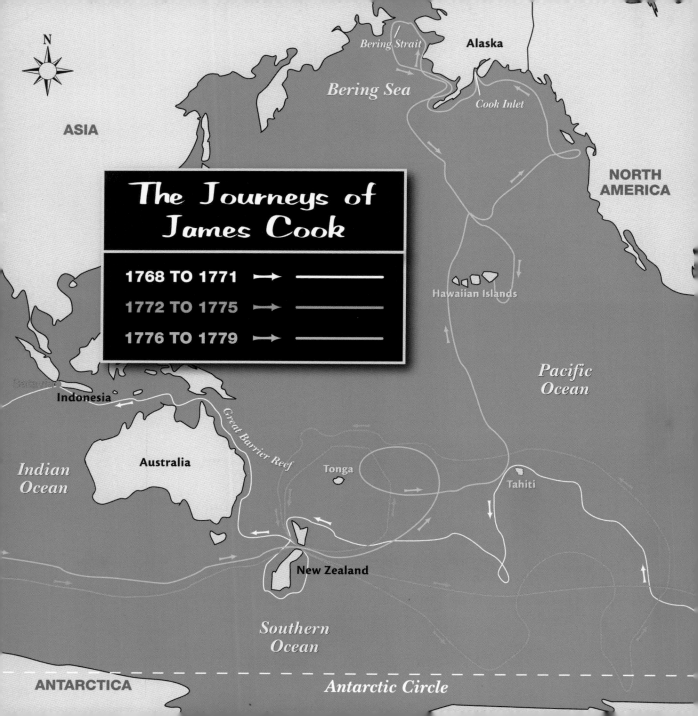

N

ASIA

Bering Strait

Alaska

Bering Sea

Cook Inlet

NORTH
AMERICA

# The Journeys of
# James Cook

| 1768 TO 1771 | ⟶ | —— |
| 1772 TO 1775 | ⟶ | —— |
| 1776 TO 1779 | ⟶ | —— |

Hawaiian Islands

Pacific
Ocean

Batavia

Indonesia

Great Barrier Reef

Indian
Ocean

Australia

Tonga

Tahiti

New Zealand

Southern
Ocean

ANTARCTICA

Antarctic Circle

England

Whitby

Plymouth

EUROPE

Labrador

Newfoundland

Quebec City

St. Lawrence River

Atlantic Ocean

Hispaniola

Cape Verde Islands

AFRICA

Indian Ocean

SOUTH AMERICA

Atlantic Ocean

Antarctic Circle

ANTARCTICA

# Final Voyage

Cook became known as the world's greatest navigator. The royalty of England knew there would be no better man for their toughest mission. Captain Cook was asked to find the fabled **Northwest Passage**.

The *Resolution* and the *Discovery* set sail from Plymouth, England, on July 12, 1776. On the way to the North Pacific, Cook revisited New Zealand, Tonga, and Tahiti.

In January 1778, Cook and his crew became the first Europeans to record the Hawaiian Islands. Explorers from Spain, Holland, and Japan may have sailed through the area as early as the 1500s. However, the islands had remained unknown to the rest of the world until Cook's landing.

**Natives on the Hawaiian coast greet Cook.**

1813
John C. Frémont born

1842
Frémont's first independent surveying mission

1820
Boone died

**Cook charted much of Hawaii's coastline.**

Five weeks after leaving the Hawaiian Islands, Cook neared the coast of present-day Oregon. The crew continued north in search of a passage to the Atlantic Ocean. Cook was disappointed when the coastline started to turn west, rather than north or east toward the Atlantic.

Farther along the Alaskan coast, Cook became hopeful once again. He noted an inlet, which he called the Gulf of Good Hope. A short time later, the inlet was determined to be a dead end. Today, it is known as Cook Inlet.

The ships eventually entered the Bering Sea. They sailed the Bering Strait, which separates Asia and North America. Following this, the expedition entered the Arctic Ocean. Here, ice blocked their way. They were forced to turn back.

At this point, Cook announced a return to Hawaii. He intended to spend the winter there, and return to the Arctic Ocean in the summer. Perhaps then the crew could explore it further.

**1856**
Frémont ran for president of the United States but lost

**1845-1846**
Frémont explored the Great Basin and the Pacific Coast, fought in the Mexican War

**1890**
Frémont died

# Would You?

Would you travel all the way back to Hawaii to wait for spring? Do you think Cook should have landed closer to the Bering Sea?

Ice in the Arctic region halted Cook's search for the Northwest Passage.

1910
Jacques Cousteau born

1951
Cousteau's first expedition in the Red Sea

1942
Cousteau and Gagnan developed the Aqua-Lung for diving

# Last Days

In January 1779, Cook's ships landed on the beaches of Hawaii. The Hawaiians greeted the crew warmly. After resting for one month, the ships set sail again. But, they soon had to return to the island because of bad weather.

Cook and his crew were not welcomed this time. The natives felt the English crew used too much of their natural resources. Many **disputes** took place.

James Cook was killed in a battle with the Hawaiian natives on February 14, 1779. The Hawaiians performed a traditional ceremony on his remains. Then, Cook's crew buried him at sea.

Without their leader, the crews of the *Discovery* and the *Resolution* were

**The battle with native Hawaiians, which took Captain Cook's life**

*1997*
Cousteau died

*1974*
Cousteau formed the Cousteau Society to protect marine life

disheartened. Still, they sailed north again to explore the Bering Strait along Asia's coast. Once again, ice forced the crew to turn back. The ships returned to England in October 1780.

Captain James Cook did not live to see the results of his work. However, his voyages provided massive amounts of information about the world's geography. And, he disproved myths about a mystery continent and a **Northwest Passage**.

**This Cook statue stands in Christchurch, New Zealand.**

# Glossary

**accurate** - free of errors.

**ammunition** - bullets, shells, and other items used in firearms.

**apprentice** - a person who learns a trade or craft from a skilled worker.

**dispute** - a forceful argument.

**fleet** - a group of ships under one command.

**master** - a person in command of a vessel.

**Northwest Passage** - a passage by sea between the Pacific and Atlantic oceans along the north coast of North America.

**scurvy** - a fatal disease caused by lack of vitamin C.

**shoal** - a sandbar or sandbank that is visible at low tide.

**survey** - to measure a piece of land to determine its shape, area, and boundaries.

# Saying It

**Batavia** - bah-TAH-vee-ah
**collier** - KAHL-yuhr
**Labrador** - LA-bruh-dawr
**Maori** - MOWR-ee
**Tahiti** - tuh-HEET-ee

# Web Sites

To learn more about James Cook, visit ABDO Publishing Company on the World Wide Web at **www.abdopub.com**. Web sites about James Cook are featured on our Book Links page. These links are routinely monitored and updated to provide the most current information available.

# Index